ELIZABETH CARY
Writer of Conscience

World Writers

ELIZABETH CARY
Writer of Conscience

Ginger Roberts Brackett

MORGAN
REYNOLDS
Incorporated

Greensboro

ELIZABETH CARY *Writer of Conscience*

Copyright © 1996 by Ginger Roberts Brackett

Photo credits: cover, frontispiece, pp. 37, 65, 77, 85-National Portrait Gallery, London;
p.13-National Trust/Art Resource, NY; p.19-The Pierpoint Morgan Library/Art Resource,
NY PML 5122 f.alr; pp. 21, 51, 55-Alinari/Art Resource, NY; pp. 23, 27-Snark, Art
Resource, NY; p. 49-Foto Marburg/Art Resource, NY.

Library of Congress Cataloging-in-Publication Data
Brackett, Ginger Roberts, 1950-
  Elizabeth Cary: writer of conscience / Ginger Roberts Brackett.
    p. cm. -- (World Writers)
  Includes bibliographical references and index.
  ISBN 1-883846-15-3
    1. Cary, Elizabeth, Lady, 1585 or 6-1639—Biography. 2. Women dramatists,
English—Early modern, 1500-1700—Biography. Women and literature—England—
History—17th century.   I. Title II. Series
PR2499.F3Z55   1996
822'.3—dc20
[B]

                                                              96-21120
                                                                  CIP

Printed in the United States of America
First Edition

*In Memory of
My Mother,
Helen Kost Roberts Ferranti,
with great gratitude and love.*

CONTENTS

Elizabeth Cary, Viscountess Falkland.

CHAPTER ONE

House Arrest

The quiet of the tiny house in Essex unsettled Elizabeth Cary. It was so different from the large London house she had shared with her family. Her new home had one room, an earthen floor and was furnished with a flock bed and an old hamper. She and Bessie, her servant and friend, used the hamper as a table when they had food to eat. Beside the makeshift table sat a single stool.

The year was 1627 and Elizabeth Cary, Viscountess Falkland, was 42 years old. She had been placed under house arrest by King Charles I on the request of her husband. Her crime was following her own conscience and deciding to convert to Catholicism during an era of intense and often brutal religious controversy.

After Elizabeth's formal conversion to Catholicism, her husband, Henry Cary, Viscount Falkland, had taken their children from her. Henry was a Protestant and had rejected the teachings of the Catholic Church. He served as Lord Deputy of Ireland, a prestigious job for a courtier—someone who served the King in various official jobs—and he was anxious to retain his good standing with the Protestant Charles I.

Elizabeth's conversion was politically dangerous to herself and to her family. Ever since King Henry VIII had created the Church of England decades before, it had been at odds with the Roman Catholic faith. The Protestant majority had ways of making Catholics suffer.

Sitting in the tiny house, Elizabeth wondered about her future for another reason. Women didn't have many legal rights in England. She could not force her husband to give her money. She had no income of any kind and could barely feed herself and Bessie, whom she often sent to eat with a friend. But she had faith that God would reward her for her sufferings.

Elizabeth did not give way to despair. She had deep inner resources to draw upon. In addition to being a wife and the mother of eleven children, Elizabeth was also a writer who was not going to allow the oppression to keep her away from her work. Alone in the tiny, cold house, she took out paper and pen and began writing a history of a king who had ruled England long ago. His name was Edward II, and he was a weak ruler who lost the loyalty of the English people. In the preface Elizabeth wrote, "To out-run those weary hours of a deep and sad passion, my melancholy pen fell accidentally on this Historical Relation; which speaks a King." Women were not supposed to be writers in seventeenth century England. Elizabeth Cary knew that women who wanted to engage in any creative activity other than sewing had been fighting public opinion for centuries. Females were considered weak-willed and stupid; incapable of learning, and evil. Some people believed that women lacked souls. Others said that females craved constant sexual satisfaction. Such ideas were based upon medical theories that claimed women easily became disturbed, which caused their wombs to travel about their bodies. Many illnesses women suffered were termed *hysteria*, a word derived from the Greek term for womb. Thus, many illnesses were blamed on women's characters, rather than on disease or infection.

If women inherited property, it automatically belonged to their husbands or sons. In a time when marriages were often arranged, especially within the upper class, women could be matched as wives with men they didn't know. This is how Elizabeth came to be married to Henry. One man wrote that "it becometh not a maid to talk, where her father and mother be in communication about her marriage, but to leave all that care and charge wholly unto them, which love her as well as herself doth." Women were to remain silent and obedient, even when they disagreed with choices made about their futures.

In her history of Edward II, Elizabeth wrote about the inequality between men and women. While a man could divorce his wife for any reason, a woman could not divorce her husband. She had no right to legal protest if he beat her. One book written to advise women and men of how they should behave said: "The world has little profit by women, but for the getting of children. But the same is not true for men, which govern Cities, armies, and do so many other weighty matters."

This negative attitude toward women persisted even though Elizabeth I, one of England's most successful leaders, had ruled England while Elizabeth Cary was a child. Queen Elizabeth had a difficult role to fulfill. She knew powerful males were closely observing her actions. They waited to proclaim her, as a woman, too weak and not intelligent enough to sit on the throne of England. How surprised Queen Elizabeth's critics must have been when she later inspired her troops to defeat the powerful Spanish Armada!

This was the environment in which Elizabeth Cary matured. The end of the sixteenth century remained a confusing time for women. While they were told of their

Elizabeth I ruled successfully, despite the resistance she met from many of her male subjects.

importance as wives and mothers, they were also made to feel inferior to men.

Sitting in that tiny house, Elizabeth Cary was determined to continue writing and worshipping as she thought right. Her writing gave her the hope that she would be able to change society's attitudes toward women. She refused to be diverted by injustice.

Elizabeth dipped her pen in the ink and began writing.

CHAPTER TWO

A Girl of Much Spirit

Elizabeth Tanfield was probably born in 1585 in Oxfordshire, England. She was an only child. Her mother, who was also named Elizabeth, was a demanding and strict woman who made her daughter kneel before speaking to her. Elizabeth's father, Lawrence Tanfield, was a lawyer highly respected for his honesty. He allowed young Elizabeth to borrow books from his library and loved to hear her read aloud. Elizabeth was lucky to have an educated parent who owned books. This was a rarity in the sixteenth century.

Elizabeth began learning French at the age of four. Later, she taught herself Spanish, Italian, and Hebrew. Once, after meeting a man from Transylvania, she decided to learn his language as well.

Elizabeth had talents in other areas. Girls were expected to learn housekeeping, with needlework to be their most important activity. She was very skillful at needlework.

As a child Elizabeth was always asking questions. She often read all night after going to bed. Her mother finally forbade the servants to give Elizabeth candles for reading. But this did not stop her. Although she had no money of her own, she secretly offered the servants money to sneak candles in to her. She presented the servants with I.O.U.s that she agreed to pay on her wedding day. True to her promise, she paid the servants close to one hundred pounds when she was married.

There were no children's books for her to read at night— they did not exist then. Few fairy tales or children's adventure stories had been recorded. Elizabeth read religious books, poetry, romances, and tales of monsters and knights battling for honor. Although these books were considered improper reading, Elizabeth was not the type of girl to let others' opinions stop her from reading what she liked.

She also read widely in the works left by the ancient Greek and Roman writers. Elizabeth lived during the Renaissance, a period when interest in the ancient world was high and a time of unprecedented creativity in England. William Shakespeare, Ben Jonson, and Christopher Marlowe thrilled people with their plays and poetry. Elizabeth may have seen Shakespeare act in one of his plays, or Queen Elizabeth I perform in one of Ben Jonson's masques, the amateur theatrical productions staged at court. The Renaissance was not enjoyed equally by all people. The majority of the poor people in London or in the countryside went about their lives of hard work and little reward. While boys who could afford it were sent to school, girls were expected to stay home and learn how to become good wives. Many women never learned to read because this was not considered a necessary skill for a wife and mother. Eventually, women were allowed to learn to read, but the men in charge of the education system had firm ideas on what a woman should be allowed to study. The belief was that women had "unstable natures." One man wrote: "Woman's thought is swift, and for the most part, unstable, walking and wandering out from home, and some will slide because of their own slipperiness." Slipperiness meant that women could not control their behavior. Women needed to be cared for, like children. They were expected to remain silent outside of the home. A woman's modesty was considered to be her highest possession. To speak in front of anyone other than family was considered rude.

Women were not to try writing anything original. They should spend their time copying the words of men. The only thing generally accepted for women to write were "mother advice books" that were necessary because so many women died during childbirth during this time of little medical knowledge. The little books provided instructions to their unborn children in case the mother died and could not share the knowledge personally.

The few women who did write books, poetry or plays usually did not sign their works. Signing a work was immodest—and no woman wished to be thought immodest. Some women placed initials on works, a practice which confused later scholars attempting to determine who wrote what. This confusion is complicated because few women's works were published. During the Renaissance, writers paid to have their works published. Few women had control of enough money to pay the expense of publication. Their works were usually passed around among friends in manuscript form.

None of these restraints on women's creativity discouraged Elizabeth. In her early teens, in an effort to impress her great uncle, Sir Henry Lee, she translated her first work. The book was *Le Miroir du Monde (The Mirror of the World),* a French work of geography written by Abraham Ortelius. Working on the translation allowed Elizabeth's imagination to travel far away from her home in Oxfordshire. She wrote that America "is not certainly known whether it be compassed with the sea, or joined to Asia on the north side." At that time geographers weren't certain how to map the New World. When she referred to Ireland as a barbarous

Elizabeth may have seen William Shakespeare acting in one of his plays.

land where people valued "liberty more than riches," she had no idea that she would someday live in that island nation, and that she too would always value freedom more than money.

Much of Elizabeth's reading was about religion. There was a great debate during these years about the nature of Christianity. After almost a thousand years of most Christians in Western Europe accepting the Roman Catholic Church's views on how to live and worship, new religious ideas had begun to gain converts in the decades before Elizabeth's birth.

While some of the new Protestant (Protestant was the name given to the non-Catholic Christian groups) leaders were motivated by theological differences, others were guided by more personal reasons. King Henry VIII had broken English Christians away from the Catholic Church because he wanted the Pope to grant him a divorce so he could marry Anne Boleyn, who later became Queen Elizabeth I's mother. When the Pope refused to end the marriage, Henry formed the Church of England. The change upset many of Henry's subjects, who wanted to remain Catholic but were forbidden to do so.

While Henry's church resembled the Catholic Church in many ways, other Protestant leaders had strong anti-Catholic opinions regarding how Christians should believe and

Henry VIII created the Church of England because the Pope would not grant him a divorce from his wife.

worship. One such Protestant leader was John Calvin, who lived and wrote in Geneva, Switzerland. In her early teens Elizabeth read a book by Calvin, who was a fierce enemy of any religious idea he thought tainted by Catholicism. She disagreed with many of his ideas and discussed them fervently with her father, who later remarked, "This girl hath a spirit averse from Calvin."

Elizabeth continued to study and read throughout her adolescence. Lawyer Tanfield appreciated his daughter's intelligence and took her to court with him as he officiated over cases. Once Elizabeth helped to prove the innocence of a woman who had confessed to being a witch. Elizabeth believed the woman confessed only because she was frightened by the court experience. Whispering to her father, Elizabeth proposed that he ask the woman if she had killed a man named John Symondes with one of her magic spells. The woman answered yes, that she had killed him. When Lawyer Tanfield pointed out that Symondes, who was Elizabeth's uncle, was alive and in the courtroom, the woman explained that she had been threatened with punishment if she didn't confess and promised mercy if she did. The woman was set free. Elizabeth's wit had bested that of the officials.

Elizabeth had tutors as she matured. One may have been Michael Drayton, a famous poet who often earned his living

E BILD
AL
O P.
ENF

NVS IC
VINI
PFARI
IN SO

N HVSS HAT DIE BEHMEN BKER
VTHER HAT DIE DEVTZSCHEN

John Calvin created an austere form of Protestant Christianity.

as a tutor. He dedicated two works that praise her talent for languages. Dedications were common ways for a writer to please patrons who could give the artist money to continue his writing career. Drayton said that Elizabeth, who would have been around ten when the dedication was written, was "adorned" with "many rare perfections." He continued: "Sweete is the French tongue, more sweete the Italian, but most sweete are they both if spoken by your admired self."

Elizabeth Tanfield was born lucky in many ways. She had a father who encouraged her to learn and to expand her imaginative horizons. He paid tutors to teach his daughter subjects other women knew little about. Her intelligence allowed her to participate in life in a way other girls could only dream of. But Elizabeth was a woman, which meant society had established certain roles that she could not avoid. One of these roles was wife. As Elizabeth turned sixteen, it was time for her to marry.

CHAPTER THREE

The Tragedy of Mariam

Elizabeth Tanfield married Henry Cary in 1602. Like many marriages of the time, it was arranged by her parents. She barely knew Cary, who was seven years older. He was a courtier, who served first Queen Elizabeth and, after her death in 1603, the new King, James I. It is doubtful that Cary loved the short, plump Elizabeth Tanfield. But she was going to inherit property from her father, and Henry needed money. The Tanfields wanted Elizabeth to marry Henry Cary because of his connections to royalty. Elizabeth, who was brought up to respect the authority of her parents, did not object to the marriage. She even vowed to be a good wife.

After the marriage, Elizabeth didn't live with her husband for several years. At first he was traveling abroad in his position as courtier. Later, Henry was taken prisoner while fighting in the Netherlands. He remained captive until a ransom was paid for his release.

While Henry was gone, Elizabeth was not allowed to write him letters. Instead, her parents hired a professional letter writer. Elizabeth was already having doubts about the Protestant faith. Her parents may have been concerned that Elizabeth would share her doubts with her new husband. They also may have been afraid for Henry to learn of his new bride's strong will. When she did at last get to write her own letters, Henry was astounded at their high quality.

After the wedding, Elizabeth lived with Henry's mother, Dame Katherine. Elizabeth's mother-in-law thought the entire household should work to satisfy her every wish. Elizabeth refused to give in to the older woman's demands. Dame Katherine retaliated by having Elizabeth locked in her room and by having all her books and writing implements confiscated. But Elizabeth had a friend who sneaked pens and paper to her. The new friend was the wife of Henry's brother, who was also named Elizabeth Cary.

It was during this time that Elizabeth wrote her first major work, a play entitled *The Tragedy of Mariam, Faire Queen of Jewry*. Elizabeth dedicated the play to her sister-in-law, which, because of their names, later caused great confusion over who was the actual author.

Mariam is a closet drama, meant to be read aloud by a group instead of performed on stage. These plays were often

King James I succeeded Elizabeth I as the first Stuart king of England.

read aloud by groups of women interested in literature. This provided a way for women to make their writing public and allowed them to take on acting roles. This could never happen on an actual stage, where even the female parts, such as those written by Shakespeare, were acted by young boys dressed in female costume.

Mariam, the hero of Elizabeth's play, was a Jewish princess of the royal family of Jerusalem. She lived about thirty years before the birth of Christ. Elizabeth probably took the story from Josephus, an ancient Jewish historian.

Mariam was married to King Herod, whom the Romans had appointed as the King of the Jews. Herod divorced his first wife to marry the beautiful Mariam. While he desired her for his wedding bed, Herod also knew the marriage would ease his way to absolute control of all the Jews.

The play is highly complicated, full of plots and sub-plots revolving around Herod's ruthless actions to gain power, such as the murder of Mariam's brother and grandfather.

Another character in the play is Herod's sister, Salome. While Mariam is good, Salome is evil. One of Salome's complaints is that men may divorce their wives, but women can't divorce their husbands. This is a circumstance that had not changed in Elizabeth's time. Women still could not divorce their husbands.

Eventually, as the title suggests, Mariam is made to

The title page of Elizabeth's first major work, *The Tragedy of Mariam, Faire Queen of Jewry.*

suffer. As in all tragedies written during the Renaissance, the main character dies because of the plotting of others and because of a flaw within herself that she does not recognize. Mariam's flaw is that she believes other people are as good as she is. Ironically, Mariam is the only character in the story who does not commit a crime.

Mariam is brought to her end by a complicated series of maneuvers carried out by Salome and Doris, the woman Herod divorced to marry Mariam. Mariam's "crime" is complaining publicly about her husband. The first line of the play foreshadows how Mariam will bring on her own end: "How oft have I with public voice run on?" When Herod returns from a trip to Rome he is told that his wife had publicly spoken of Herod's murder of her grandfather and her brother. He is also upset by the cool reception he receives from his wife. But he tells her that if she will only smile he will forgive her. He even promises to bring her riches and gold from the temple. But Mariam tells him that the only thing that will make her smile would be the return of her brother and grandfather. At this time, Salome accuses Mariam of being unfaithful to Herod, and Herod is told that his wife is planning to poison him. Herod orders her executed.

Mariam dies protesting her innocence. Herod goes mad after the execution because of his guilt at having her killed.

Elizabeth's play seems to be a warning to Renaissance women to be careful in their behavior. As a young woman living without her husband, Elizabeth probably thought a great deal about marriage. Her culture expected certain behaviors from females. Attitudes toward women had changed little since the time of Mariam. Elizabeth had written a "cautionary" tale, warning women of the trouble they would encounter if they failed to follow the conventions of their society.

Mariam was written in 1602 or 1603, but was not made public until 1612. However, Elizabeth's friends probably passed the play around and read it aloud in front of audiences before its publication.

Elizabeth may have written several other works as she waited for Henry to return from abroad. After Elizabeth's death, her daughter wrote about several plays her mother had written. One was a companion play to *Mariam* set on the island of Syracuse. All of these works are lost. But Elizabeth had other works yet to write.

CHAPTER FOUR

Marriage and Motherhood

While she waited for Henry's return from captivity in the Netherlands, Elizabeth continued to have doubts about her Protestant religion. Henry's brother Aldolphus, who spoke positively of the Catholic faith, urged her to read about it. Elizabeth read all she could find written in French, Spanish and Italian about the Catholic faith.

This was an era when many people were asking questions about the nature of religious belief. Even Protestants disagreed about the correct way to worship. What had begun under King Henry VIII as the Church of England eventually divided informally into the High Church, which believed in a great deal of ritual during worship services, and the Low Church, which believed that the rituals of the High Church were too much like the Catholic mass. Each Protestant group requested that the king support them. This squabbling soon led to divisions in the Church of England. Another group, the Puritans, inspired by the writings of John Calvin, formed their own sect. In their eyes, the Church of England had become non-spiritual. They demanded an austere worship service and changes in the central doctrine of the Church. The Puritans were harassed almost as much as the Catholics. Consequently, many left England, moving first to Holland, before traveling to the English colonies in the New World. Later in the seventeenth century, these religious disagreements would be one of the causes of the bloody English Civil War.

Elizabeth observed all of this religious disagreement with interest. A spiritual woman, her faith was important. Eventually, she stopped attending formal church services. Instead, she visited with church leaders in their homes and invited them to her own, in search of guidance.

Henry was finally released from prison after an expensive ransom was paid. After his return Elizabeth, who had no children for the first seven years of her marriage, bore eleven babies. Her first child was born in 1609 and named Catherine. When Elizabeth's first son, Lucius, was born a year later, he was removed to be raised by her parents, who had no son of their own. This was a common practice among the upper classes. Just because it was common, did not mean that the mothers of these babies liked it. King James I's own wife, Queen Anne, protested when her husband wanted their son to be raised by wealthy relatives. Although the queen protested, the prince was taken from her.

Between the years of 1613 and 1625, nine more children were born: Lorenzo, Victoria, Anne, Edward (who died as an infant), Elizabeth, Lucy, Mary, Patrick, and Henry.

After the children began arriving, Henry and Elizabeth moved into a house of their own, and Elizabeth kept busy caring for her home and family. She taught the first four children herself, then turned that job over to tutors. The boys attended school when old enough. As religious faith was most important to her, Elizabeth was careful to instruct her children in Christianity. However, she chose not to use the normal instruction book, called a catechism. Instead, she tried to teach them by example. She made clear to her children that everything they had was a gift from God. They knew early on that, according to Elizabeth, even the King was God's servant.

When she was pregnant with her fourth child, Victoria, Elizabeth became ill. In those days, many women died in childbirth. She assumed that might happen to her. She wrote her own mother's advice book, instructing her children in the subjects she would have liked to teach them. Happily, she did not die and lived to teach her children herself.

As a wealthy wife of a member of the court, Elizabeth was expected to dress in stylish fashions. Henry had become angry with her once for not dressing as suited her rank. Having little interest in her appearance, and considering dressing a torture, she turned her personal appearance over to her ladies-in-waiting. Elizabeth became very impatient while her servants prepared her to meet the public. Pacing, deep in thought, Elizabeth caused her maids to chase after her in order to fasten a pin or braid her hair.

Even though Elizabeth took little pleasure in caring for her looks or dress, she enjoyed dressing her children and making sure they enjoyed recreation. Learning to direct her servants and care for her household became her major occupation, surprising those who knew her bookish ways. During this busy time, she seemed to have stopped writing, although she likely continued to read as much as possible.

Obedience to Henry was difficult for Elizabeth. She often found obeying anyone else difficult. But she knew what must be her role in the family and in society. Elizabeth urged the children to love their father more than they loved her, and she tried to share in Henry's activities. Even though she was frightened by horses, Elizabeth learned to ride at Henry's urging. Such activity was critical to advancing Henry's career at court. During one pregnancy, Elizabeth fell off as her horse was leaping a hedge and a ditch. At first, other riders believed her dead, but she recovered and later delivered a healthy baby. After that accident, Henry became sympathetic to his wife's fears. He no longer forced Elizabeth to join him in riding.

Henry Cary had money problems his entire life. He often spent beyond his means and later blamed Elizabeth for his poverty. With an aristocratic household to maintain, and ten children to care for, Elizabeth likely did spend a great deal of money. She was also absent-minded, and probably didn't do a good job of bookkeeping.

When Elizabeth's children were young, Henry asked her to mortgage the property her father had given her when she married. That meant the property would be lost if they couldn't repay the loan. She agreed, but this so angered her father that he disinherited her altogether. Instead of Elizabeth, her son Lucius became his heir.

Elizabeth often became depressed. At one point, while pregnant, Elizabeth ate nothing other than toast and a little beer (a common drink in those days) for two weeks. She told those around her that she could no longer feel her child moving within, and they feared it might have died. However, she came out of this bout of depression and delivered a healthy child. She had several more bouts with depression, but resisted talking about her sadness. She also suffered from headaches and would sleep to be rid of them. This may be what prompted her, at the time she wrote *Mariam*, to describe Herod as sleeping when he suffered from head-

Queen Anne protested the tradition of having the eldest son raised outside the home.

aches. Writers often include details from their own lives in their stories. She also learned that it eased her own pain by helping others relieve their worries. She was usually affectionate and sympathetic toward her friends and family.

When Henry became Controller of the King's Household, they had to live at court. About this time, Henry's father died, and his mother and some sisters came to live with them. Because of the increase in the size of her family, and due to her new court responsibilities, Elizabeth turned the housework over to others. Although still a Protestant, Elizabeth continued to study Catholicism. She grew to admire Mary, the mother of Jesus. Pregnant again, Elizabeth decided that if her child was a daughter, she would name her for Mary. Elizabeth's daughter, Mary Cary, born in 1621, would become a nun in the Catholic Church.

Elizabeth's life changed again when Henry was appointed Deputy Minister of Ireland in 1622. Elizabeth had once labeled Ireland barbaric. But now she, along with her six youngest children, was going to live in that turbulent, Catholic island nation.

CHAPTER FIVE

The Deed Is Done

Henry Cary, Lord Falkland, served as Deputy Minister in Ireland from 1622 until 1629. He was in charge of making sure the Irish obeyed the laws of the English king. This office was an advancement in Henry's career.

While Henry busied himself with the legal aspects of Ireland, Elizabeth set about trying to improve people's lives. She had a plan to help the desperately poor Irish help themselves. She designed an enterprise to employ skilled craftsmen, such as weavers of wool and linen, dyers, spinners, knitters, hatters, lace makers and others. These artisans, or masters, would teach the children their various crafts. In this way, the children could earn a living. At the same time they would be using products from Ireland. That would help the country better support itself.

She chose around 160 children, most older than seven

years. Previously, the children had spent their days begging. Separated into several rooms in several buildings, the apprenticed girls and boys worked with their teachers. They were divided according to the tasks. Large strong boys did tasks requiring strength, while girls participated in more sedentary activities, such as spinning and sewing. The project produced a broadcloth so fine that her own husband, the highest legal official in the country, wore it.

Unfortunately, Elizabeth was not very skilled at running a business. She allowed herself to be distracted when keeping her accounts and had a poor memory in matters of business. She often didn't even record the payments she made and sometimes paid the same bill more than once, even up to five times. The persons receiving payments did not alert her to this fact, but kept the multiple payments. Many of her workers proved to be dishonest and took advantage of her lack of planning skills. When observers tried to caution her against the dishonesty of those with whom she worked, she ignored their advice.

Elizabeth's daughter described her as being possessed with a great energy when carrying out projects such as the Irish venture. Elizabeth became so focused on her goal she ignored everything else. She would pawn an item, giving it to someone who would loan her money until she could buy it back, then find she needed that same item only a hour later. Her enthusiasm also led her to make promises she wasn't able to keep. After gaining a bit of perspective on such situations, following the passage of time, Elizabeth could look back and see her mistakes. She could not, unfortunately, seem to avoid those mistakes at the time she committed them.

The enterprise also suffered from natural disasters. One storehouse suffered damage in a fire. Eventually out of funds and low on materials, Elizabeth had to admit that her project had failed.

While in Ireland, Elizabeth made the acquaintance of a Catholic priest. She admired his learning and judgment. His faith impressed Elizabeth enough that she began to seriously consider converting to Catholicism. She knew this decision would radically alter her life, and the lives of her husband and children. Ever one to try to educate herself regarding subjects in which she was interested, she searched out those who had switched from Catholicism to Protestantism. She hoped to learn what problems others had with the faith. She learned of one such convertee who served Henry Cary as a chaplain. When Elizabeth asked him about his change in religion, he explained the switch was due to his frustrated career plans. While a member of the Catholic clergy, he wanted to go to Rome. Church officials told him he had to stay in his homeland of Scotland instead. Because this displeased him, he chose to leave the church. The decision had little to do with Elizabeth's own questions of faith. She continued to wonder which was the better of the two faiths for her.

The births of the two youngest children, both sons, occurred while Elizabeth lived in Ireland. After three years away, Elizabeth decided to make a trip back to England, taking her eldest unmarried daughter along with the three youngest children. The others remained with Henry.

On the ship, during a violent storm on the voyage to England, Elizabeth and her infant son were struck by a wave which seemed to take the baby's breath away. All the travelers believed him to be dead. But he finally began to breathe again.

In England, Elizabeth took the children to her mother's house rather than going to London, because the plague, which struck the city several times during these years, was raging.

One of the reasons Elizabeth had come home to England was to visit Catherine, her eldest daughter. Catherine had married four years earlier at age thirteen and was a great favorite with her husband's family. Elizabeth once asked her daughter why her mother-in-law loved her so. Although she said she was not sure, Catherine believed it was due to the fact that she had always followed Elizabeth's advice in how to deal with others. Elizabeth told Catherine when she married to always obey the will of others over her own, as long as she could do so in good conscience and if their requests seemed reasonable. For Elizabeth to add these conditions reflected her own intellect. While more than willing to comply with others, she would not compromise or endanger her own ideals and beliefs.

When Catherine, who was about six months pregnant, came to visit Elizabeth and her sisters and brothers, a footman tried to carry her across a narrow bridge. He fell on the slippery surface, and both he and Catherine plunged into the water. Attempting to block her fall, the footman managed to get underneath her. Catherine insisted she was not injured or frightened, but that night she became ill. By the end of the week Catherine was dying, and the baby was born three months early. Elizabeth stayed by her daughter's side throughout the ordeal. She promised Catherine that she would nurse her new grandchild along with her infant son, but the baby died along with his mother.

Elizabeth didn't give way publicly to her grief. She took comfort from a vision Catherine had before she died. She told those around her that she saw beside her bed a "bright woman clothed in white having a crown on her head." Elizabeth became convinced that Catherine had had a vision of the Virgin Mary, and that Catherine had been a Catholic when she died.

After the plague had passed, Elizabeth and her children went to London. Taking it upon herself to try to better the financial circumstances for her husband and others, she wrote some letters to the King's secretary, Lord Conway. This was common practice at that time. Such letters usually asked for financial support, or pleaded for one side or another of a lawsuit.

Elizabeth also visited with a Catholic bishop and invited "divines," or people well versed in religion, to come to her house to exchange ideas. Such intellectual meetings caught the attention of citizens of the aristocracy, and soon many well-known people were visiting with Elizabeth and her friends. She became friends with Lord Ormande, a man who had been imprisoned for his Catholic beliefs under King James I. He would remain Elizabeth's friend and helper for life.

Lady Denby, a good friend of Elizabeth's, joined the discussions. She told Elizabeth that she, too, was interested in the Catholic religion, and that she was thinking of converting. She promised Elizabeth that they could convert together, but each time they planned to do so, Lady Denby would fail to show up. Finally, Elizabeth went to court to find Lady Denby and to discover if she was seriously considering converting. But Lady Denby had laid a trap.

She told Elizabeth, "Well, I have you now in the court and here I will keep you. You shall lie in my chamber and shall not go forth." Lady Denby planned to keep Elizabeth at court to keep her from converting.

Because she thought it best to pretend to go along with Lady Denby, Elizabeth did not protest. She acted contented with her friend's plan, fooling Lady Denby into leaving her alone, then seized the opportunity and escaped to the home of Lord Ormande.

At Lord Ormande's, Elizabeth met a Catholic priest she had been talking to regarding the conversion. A short time later, in Lord Ormande's stable, Elizabeth Cary, Viscountess Falkland, took a vow of Catholicism. After all her years of doubt, in 1626, at the age of forty, she finally made the decision to become a Catholic. Then she did a rather amazing thing. Elizabeth returned to the court and found Lady Denby. She told her one-time friend that she was now content to stay with her for as long as she pleased, because "the deed was done."

CHAPTER SIX

The History of Edward II

Lady Denby was troubled by Elizabeth's conversion to Catholicism. She appealed to her brother, the powerful Duke of Buckingham, to help her convince Elizabeth to return to Protestantism. But Elizabeth turned a deaf ear to their pleas. Frustrated, Buckingham went directly to King Charles I with news of Elizabeth's change of faith.

Buckingham had been a favorite of the recently deceased King James I. Their friendship had been so close that many suspected them of being lovers. Buckingham was also a favorite of Charles I, although no one hinted of sexual relations between them. Most feared and respected the power and influence Buckingham held at court. Henry Cary, for example, depended on the aid of Buckingham to assist him in his dealings with the court. If anyone could convince the King to use his royal power to persuade Elizabeth to renounce Catholicism, it would be Buckingham.

Elizabeth also had a powerful friend at court—the Queen. A French princess when she married Charles I, Henrietta Maria was Catholic. Charles may have wished for a Protestant wife, but this marriage was arranged to help keep the nations of England and France, which had a long history of warring with one another, at peace. It is possible that Henrietta Maria's influence restrained her husband from imposing an even more severe punishment on Elizabeth.

Charles allowed Elizabeth to leave the court but placed her under house arrest. This meant she could not leave her home. The King hoped the isolation would convince Elizabeth to change her mind. No known Catholic could come near her; all of her household members were Protestant.

The Protestant preacher who had earlier tutored Elizabeth visited her during her house arrest. He became so upset at her refusal to renounce Catholicism that he threw himself on the ground kicking and screaming. He told Elizabeth others would be afraid to hire him as a teacher because of her conversion. He left her house in frustration and never returned.

Henry Cary was furious with his wife. He immediately stopped sending her money. Henry feared her conversion would hurt his position at court. In December of 1626, Henry wrote to the King and asked that Elizabeth be sent to live with her mother. He thought Lady Tanfield might "save" her daughter. He thanked the King for removing his daughter Victoria from the "leprosy" of Elizabeth's influence, and referred to Catholic priests as "the locusts of Rome." He also informed everyone he knew that his marriage was a failure. He no longer wanted to be associated with Elizabeth. In one letter he referred to Elizabeth as one "whom now I may say I have long unhappily called wife."

Henry's efforts to force Elizabeth to live with her mother failed because Lady Tanfield refused to allow her daughter to stay in her childhood home. Although she never learned how to spell properly, Lady Tanfield knew how to make her feelings clear: "My desiers wass I dout not by plesying to God, to have yout to lyve with yor husband and lyve in that relegeon wherin you war bred." She told Elizabeth that she may "com not to me," and added, "I prays my god I never dyd that thing to ofend my father, and my mother, my Der, my most dere husband your most loving father." She concluded her letter by claiming that Elizabeth was ruining her own children.

While all this furor was raging about her, Elizabeth was living at home with little money. She sent her children to share meals with friends. Her living conditions had deteriorated, but she felt it was a small price to pay for her faith. Then she suffered the most painful blow of all. Her children, and all her servants, except Bessie Poulter, whom Elizabeth

King Charles I placed Elizabeth under house arrest after her conversion to Catholicism.

had raised, were moved out on Henry's command. Despite the pain of missing her children, Elizabeth never considered altering her decision.

During this time Elizabeth had no meat to eat. She often sent Bessie to eat with others. Bessie slipped bread and pie crusts into handkerchiefs to take home to Elizabeth. When Bessie could stand her mistress's condition no longer, she pleaded with Lord Ormonde to send food. Elizabeth wrote to Lord Conway and asked that her husband be forced to "give me necessary means to feed and clothe me."

Others interceded on Elizabeth's behalf. Lady Manners, the stepmother of the Duchess of Buckingham, visited Elizabeth. After witnessing the dire circumstances that she was forced to live in, Lady Manners enlisted the help of other ladies in Charles's court. They wanted others to know the conditions Elizabeth was being forced to live in because of her religious beliefs.

Elizabeth requested permission from the King to move to Essex to live near her sister. This time the King agreed to her request.

Henry Cary was dismayed that Elizabeth had been granted permission to move to Essex, which was about ten miles outside of London. He continued to write complaining letters to court, accusing Elizabeth of such bad behavior as refusing to "live quietly." When the King's privy council,

Queen Henrietta Maria was Elizabeth's most powerful friend at court.

the men charged with making legal decisions, ordered Henry to send his wife five hundred pounds a year, Henry refused—even when Charles personally ordered him to comply with the instructions.

When it became clear that her confinement, and later her banishment to Essex, was not going to force Elizabeth to reconvert to Protestantism, others began telling her she was a disgrace to her husband and that she was harming her children by remaining separated from them. Elizabeth reminded them that Henry had taken her children away. She wanted them to return to live with her.

In Essex, Elizabeth's Catholic friends could visit. She drew support and strength from their company. Her spirits were also bolstered when Bessie converted to Catholicism.

The two women seemed content in their little house, although Elizabeth desperately missed her children. During one season of Lent, Elizabeth and Bessie ate so much boiled fish that afterwards Bessie refused to ever eat the dish again. Occasionally, Elizabeth's grief at being separated from her children overwhelmed her and she would call out for them as though they were present. Bessie would be forced to remind Elizabeth that the children were with Henry. Elizabeth had always been eccentric, and during this trying time the depression she often suffered made this aspect of her character even more pronounced.

Henry finally sent Elizabeth the money the privy council had ordered. But she continued to live as an outcast from noble society. Henry was in Ireland with the children, who visited occasionally—except for the eldest son, Lucius, who took his father's side in the dispute. This was a painful period for Elizabeth. She was paying a high price for her religious beliefs. But there was one great benefit gained from her years of isolation. She began writing again—and broke down another barrier restricting women's intellectual freedom.

During the Renaissance it was not considered proper for a woman to be interested in writing history. The few women who did write were supposed to model their work on male historians and to add no new words of their own. But Elizabeth departed from this example while writing *The History of Edward II*. Clearly, there were aspects of Edward II's life story that she found too intriguing, and too relevant to her own life, to resist exploring on her own.

The writing of history had not yet been clearly separated from other types of writing, such as drama, during the seventeenth century. Much as Shakespeare used a fictional approach in his historical plays (the character Falstaff in the plays about Henry I and Henry V, for example, is entirely fictional), Elizabeth adopted some fictional techniques in her history of Edward II. She invented dialogue when there was no record of what was actually said. She expanded on ideas she knew the historical characters had held; many of the speeches that she put into the historical characters' mouths sound as though they were being spoken on stage. Some scholars are convinced she had plans to shape her history into a play similar to the works of Shakespeare, Christopher Marlowe, and Ben Jonson. She clearly loved the theater and had quite likely seen the play Marlowe had already written about the rule of Edward II.

In the history Elizabeth criticizes rulers, such as Edward, who ignore their subjects in order to satisfy their own desires. She probably intended for this criticism to serve a dual purpose. James I, who was the father of the present King Charles I, had some characteristics similar to Edward II. Both allowed themselves to be distracted from their royal duties by their homosexual attractions to other men. When Elizabeth criticized Edward for allowing his lovers to exert a powerful influence on his behavior as ruler, it could clearly be understood, especially by her contemporaries, as also being a criticism of James I, who had often let his close friend Buckingham influence his decisions as King. She may also have been motivated by the fact that Buckingham had sided with her husband in his efforts to force her to reject Catholicism.

King Charles I had the power to severely punish anyone

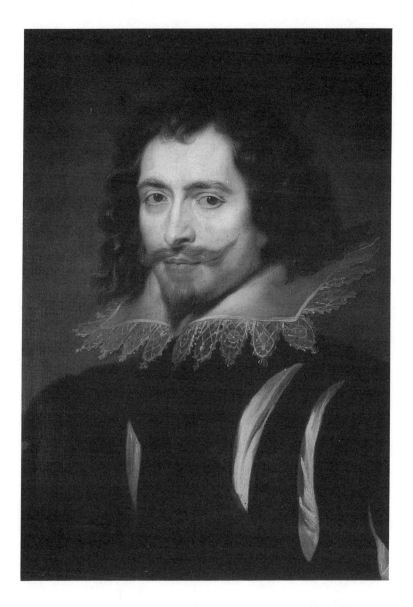

The Duke of Buckingham often influenced the decisions of his close friend King James I.

who offended him. Although Charles differed from his father in many ways and attempted to solve more problems than did James I, he was never able to find solutions to most of his nation's ills. Eventually, Charles' inability to rule effectively and his heavy-handed attempts to stamp out disagreement would result in the bloody English Civil War, and his own beheading in 1649.

Had Elizabeth tried to make her history public, she would have endangered herself and her family. She insisted on writing the truth as she saw it. In her view, Edward II's preoccupation with his male friends had made him a bad ruler.

There was also a strong female character in Elizabeth's history. Edward's wife, Isabel, left her husband, disgusted with his weak and ineffectual rule, and gathered an army in order to place their son on the throne. Isabel's actions eventually resulted in Edward II's capture, torture and execution.

Isabel had not been kindly treated by earlier, male historians. They portrayed her as wicked and scheming. The betrayal of a king was treason. For a queen to have a sexual affair with another man was punishable by death, because preserving the purity of the royal bloodline was considered the queen's most grave responsibility. Isabel, who Elizabeth points out was wife "in name only," turned for love and companionship to another man, Mortimer. While Elizabeth's version does not condone Isabel's adultery, she defends Isabel's actions by pointing out that Edward had been the first to abandon the marriage. Isabel is also portrayed as being intelligent and wily in her dealing with Edward and his favorites in the court. But Elizabeth does criticize Isabel near the end of the work. During her efforts to overthrow her husband, Isabel resorts to torture and execution of her enemies. Isabel's actions are also intensified by the unexpressed rage and desire for revenge she develops over the years of being mistreated by Edward II. Elizabeth writes that Isabel's actions were "too great and deep a blemish to suit a Queen, a Woman, and a Victor."

In the preface to *The History of Edward II*, Elizabeth says that she wrote "to out-run those weary hours of a deep and sad Passion." Perhaps she did write out of loneliness. But she also states in the preface that "I have not herein followed the dull Character of our Historians, nor amplified more than they infer, by Circumstance. I strive to please the truth, not time." In other words, she wanted to write about a subject that had been dealt with by previous historians— but she sought to do it in a more interesting way.

Whatever her reasons for writing *The History of Edward II*, Elizabeth performed a remarkable feat—another first for an English woman writer. But her writing was not yet finished. She would soon translate the forbidden works of a French Roman Catholic writer. Once again, she would ignore the rules and behave as her conscience demanded.

CHAPTER SEVEN

Defending the Faith

Although much of her time during this period of living alone was occupied with arguing her case for financial support from Henry, Elizabeth continued to write during these years. Her daughter later remarked on the many religious works, such as biographies of female saints and a hymn to the Virgin Mary, that Elizabeth had written. Most of these are lost today.

However, in 1630 Elizabeth began work on a project that would bring her even more notoriety. She decided to translate the writings of a French Catholic official, Cardinal Perron, whose works had been attacked in writing in 1620 by James I. Elizabeth wanted to defend them. She chose to openly take sides in the ongoing debate between Catholics and Protestants. Such a move could have proven dangerous to her. She was again insulting the father of the present king, Charles I—the very king she was asking to help her.

Elizabeth translated *The Reply of the Most Illustrious Cardinall of Perron* in one month. She dedicated it to Queen Henrietta Maria, the Catholic wife of Charles I. Dedications were meant to praise those people at whom they were directed. Elizabeth's dedication was no exception. She wrote that the queen was "a woeman, though farr above other woemen, therefor fittest to protect a woeman's worke." One purpose of the dedication was to ask Queen Henrietta Maria to protect her from criticism from Charles I.

The work also contains an address to the reader, called an epistle, or letter. In this epistle, Elizabeth tells her readers that she wants to be known "as a Catholic and a Woman: the first serves for mine honor, and the second, for my excuse." She defies Protestants by labeling her religion as an honor. She also makes fun of the idea that women could not write: "if the worke be but meanely done, it is noe wonder, for my Sexe can raise noe great expectation of anye thing that shall come from me. . . I will not make use of that worne-out forme of saying I printed it against my will, mooved by the importunitie of Friends." This is a reference to the excuse all women had to make if they wanted to publish their writing, in which they were forced to claim that their friends or family had coaxed them into allowing the public to see their work. Elizabeth refuses to play this role. She openly takes responsibility for her translation.

But Elizabeth saves her strongest statement for last when she writes that she has command of a language that many of the educated men of her country do not. Ironically, her translation went to Oxford University, a place women were not even allowed to enter. The epistle is a stunning support of the intellectual endeavors of a woman.

The Reply of the most Illustrious Cardinall of Perron was printed in Europe and smuggled into England. The man who occupied the highest Protestant office in England, the Archbishop of Canterbury, named George Abbot, seized and burned all but twelve copies. He also called the translation "heretical," which meant that Elizabeth had committed a religious crime. The few copies of the translation which survived were carefully preserved and stored in a safe place.

Shortly before Elizabeth began her translation, her mother died. The estate that Elizabeth should have inherited went instead to her eldest son, Lucius. While Lucius took his father's side against his mother, he did try to help her financially. She refused his help at times, while on other occasions she accepted it.

Her refusal of the financial support was curious because Elizabeth remained constantly in debt. Her daughter describes her as "rather too forward in borrowing." If someone asked Elizabeth for a loan, she would borrow money to lend to another. Never a good account keeper, she often vowed to repay loans to her creditors, then immediately forgot about them. Whenever she was reminded of her debts, she promised their repayment with sincerity. On other occasions, she was drawn into business deals in an effort to earn money. But each venture failed.

Elizabeth often left her house disorderly and unattended in order to write, tend to the needy, or engage in business. Over the years, she became more and more eccentric. Sometimes, for example, she wasn't sure whether she was cold or hungry and would call out for beer when she had burned herself at the fire. When people reminded her of her own thoughts, she cheerfully accepted their help, expressing her gratitude as though she had never heard the thought before.

Meanwhile, Henry was having a difficult time. He lost his appointment in Ireland after he tried to evict all of the Catholic priests from that very Catholic country. This politically impractical move embarrassed the King. After all, Charles had married a Catholic wife and was trying to maintain peace with France, a Catholic country. Henry was called home and, although he was still welcomed at court, never regained his high political status.

Through the efforts of Queen Henrietta Maria, Elizabeth and Henry became friendly once again, although they never shared a house together. Henry's financial conditions were grim. He had hoped their eldest son would marry a wealthy woman, the daughter of the lord treasurer, in order to bring money again into the family. But Lucius' 1630 marriage to Lettice Morison, the daughter of one of Henry's friends, brought no such fortune to the Cary family.

Elizabeth was fond of Lettice, her daughter-in-law. Lettice was a strong-minded woman who had designs to improve the lot of the poor and of females. She had a plan to institute schools for girls throughout England. Unfortunately, her plans were interrupted by the English Civil War, which broke out about twelve years after her marriage to Lucius.

During this period, Elizabeth tried to once again follow the conventions of fashion and behavior. She even slowed her efforts to help others and consulted with Henry before approaching the King for aid for herself, to be sure such an action wouldn't damage his reputation.

Ironically, Elizabeth, who herself had been at odds with Lucius, worked to reconcile Lucius and Henry. Lucius was becoming a well-known figure in English society. He followed his mother's example and became a political writer and poet. He joined a group of young men who gathered together to support and learn from the famous playwright and poet Ben Jonson. These men were called "Sons of Ben," and Jonson refers to several of them in his poetry. After Lucius assumed his father's title, becoming the Second Viscount Falkland, Ben Jonson wrote an entire poem about the death of one of Lucius' friends and the friendship they had shared.

Elizabeth also began to see her other children again. Three of her daughters and her two youngest sons had not been with their mother for several years. They felt embarrassed by her conversion and offered her little respect. But Anne, the eldest surviving daughter, remembered her mother well and took her side in disagreements with the remainder of the family. Elizabeth was careful not to try to convert her children to Catholicism. While she discussed her views on that faith, she didn't push her children toward it, for fear she might alienate them even more.

Two years after returning to England, Henry Cary suffered an accident. While hunting with the King, he fell from a hunting stand and broke his leg. His daughter wrote that, while attempting to rise to his feet in the presence of the King (which was required of all subjects), Henry's leg broke in a second and third location. Afterwards, he became very ill, suffering from an infection in his wound after a surgeon tried to set the broken bone. Elizabeth quickly traveled the twenty miles from London in order to be with Henry. She stayed at his bedside night and day, watching over him.

More doctors were called in as gangrene developed in

Poet and playwright Ben Jonson was a friend of Lucius Cary.

Henry's leg. The consulting physicians agreed that the leg needed to be removed, and Henry allowed the surgery to take place. His leg was cut off just above his knee, and his daughter wrote that he never showed any signs of pain. She vividly described the "searching" of the wound, an action to which Henry replied, "Oh, softly!" While some type of "powder" was applied to the amputation site, no "searing" with heat took place. Henry continued to bleed profusely.

His daughters and two younger sons came to see him, and Anne cried out when she saw her father suffering. Henry called them to his bedside, blessed them, and sent them home. His daughter described the following hours in moving language. According to her, the doctors did not want Henry to know of the seriousness of his condition, so they discussed it with Elizabeth in French. Henry understood their conversation, however, and supposedly asked his wife if a priest was nearby. He had decided to convert to Catholicism. No priest was near, so Elizabeth told him how to make an "internal" confession. He spoke no more as Elizabeth prayed over him. His physicians asked him to state that he died a Protestant; otherwise, with Elizabeth there, everyone might believe he had died a "papist," a Catholic. After they had repeated their request several times, Henry told them, "Pray, do not interrupt my silent meditation." One week following his accident, in 1633,

Henry, First Viscount Falkland, died of complications from his injury.

Elizabeth wept at the death of her husband, but then recovered her demeanor. As when her beloved eldest daughter and first grandchild died, Elizabeth didn't show much emotion. She borrowed a coach and took Henry's body to his house, a distance of about nine miles, where some of the daughters waited for news. Arriving at about three o'clock in the morning, she first tried to conceal Henry's death from her children. She thought it better to prepare them by telling them his condition had worsened. But they were so troubled, thinking she had left him while he was without hope, that she finally told her children of their father's death.

Elizabeth convinced her daughters to come live with her again by telling them their father would have wanted it so. Having inherited a small yearly payment upon Henry's death, Elizabeth used much of this money to repay her debts. The sale of Henry's property also brought in much-needed funds, allowing Elizabeth to plan for the future. Henry's, as well as some of Elizabeth's, acquaintances criticized her for forcing her children to live in poor conditions, rather than sending them to live with wealthy friends or relatives. She did her best to provide for the children, making sure they had food on days when she fasted.

After Henry's death, Elizabeth no longer attended the public plays she so enjoyed, nor did she appear at court for the purposes of enjoying such frivolities as the dramas known as "masques." She did go about in public and court to carry out business. Elizabeth's short, plump figure, scurrying about dressed in black, became a familiar sight to Londoners. Her two elder sons visited with her that first winter. Many of their friends, Oxford scholars and others, were welcomed to her house. Elizabeth's home became a renowned location for meetings during which intellectual and religious discussions took place. The public began to accept her eccentric ways. Also, her reputation as an intellectual, and as the mother of the poet and statesman Lucius Cary, grew. Gradually, Elizabeth's children softened their attitudes toward her. Several began to seriously consider conversion to Catholicism.

Elizabeth must have been pleased as she viewed many members of her family together once again. But all the while, she thought of her two youngest sons, who still lived with Lucius. She wanted them to attend school in Europe where they might receive an education at a Catholic institution. She knew, however, that Lucius would never agree to such a plan.

After much consideration, Elizabeth put a plan into motion to remove her youngest sons from Lucius' care. The plan involved kidnaping the boys, to whom she had no legal claims. She could be severely punished for such an action, perhaps even imprisoned in the dreaded Tower of London. Whatever thoughts of danger may have occurred to Elizabeth, she dismissed them. Elizabeth Cary never hesitated to act upon her convictions.

CHAPTER EIGHT

Patience Triumphs

Before Elizabeth could put her plan to bring her sons to come live with her into action, she found herself struggling to hold onto her daughters.

Although Elizabeth had hoped that her daughters would convert, her Catholic friends discouraged her from pressing the issue. They felt her wishes would never come true and that to continue to pursue it would only result in self-torture. But, as in all other things, Elizabeth clung to her hope for her daughters' conversions with implacable stubbornness, and eventually her dream came true. Lucy Cary was the first daughter to convert. She was influenced by a thirty-three year old priest, Father Cuthbert, who amazed even Lucius with his wit and learning. Lucy's sisters soon followed her example.

Outsiders tried to stop the daugthers' conversions. Lord Newburgh, a close friend of Henry's who had been very kind to Elizabeth, appealed to the King to command Elizabeth to send her daughters to live with Lucius before the conversions took place. This time, Elizabeth defended herself before the King. She explained the difficulty she would face in parting with her children and insisted that they were old enough to decide for themselves where they wanted to live. She called upon her knowledge of law gained from her father, and argued that the girls had done nothing which should cause their liberty to be revoked. Then she approached the problem from another direction, arguing that taking on the care of four girls would be a hardship to her son. She did not believe they should be forced against their wills to go to a brother who had not asked that they come. Her argument must have been convincing, because King Charles told her to keep her daughters until she heard from him again. Then Charles communicated with Lucius, requesting his opinion on the situation. Lucius responded that he didn't want the girls to come against their wills, as that would make his house a prison, and him their jailer.

Ironically, the dispute convinced the girls to hurry their conversions, out of fear that they would be removed from their surroundings.

In the meantime, the family was often visited by Lord Chillingworth, who Elizabeth believed to be a sound Catholic. Elizabeth had many lengthy conversations with him, and he encouraged the girls to convert. Over time, however, Chillingworth reverted back to Protestantism and suggested that the girls do the same. He attempted to gain power over them and urged them to doubt Catholic teachings. He also told the girls to go live with Lucius, who had remained a Protestant.

The daughter named after Elizabeth was almost convinced by Chillingworth to go to Lucius. But when the sisters considered all Chillingworth had said, young Elizabeth, along with the others, began to see many contradictions in his words. He seemed to be saying that he could be everything to all people, a Catholic to Catholics, and a Protestant to Protestants. Their mother had not suspected a problem with Chillingworth's honesty, as he spoke to the girls in private. She believed that he encouraged them toward Catholicism.

Elizabeth was warned by a Lord Craven, a Protestant who liked the Carys, that Chillingworth was not a Catholic. Chillingworth had also confused Lord Craven's brother by guiding him to the brink of conversion, then cautioning him against it. This caused the brother great anxiety and mental and emotional confusion. Finally, Chillingworth was told not to return to the brother's house. When Elizabeth confronted Chillingworth with these claims, he dismissed them as lies told by those who were jealous of his beliefs.

Although Elizabeth didn't know it, Chillingworth had proposed to Lord Newburgh that he again try to remove the daughters from Elizabeth's care. All the while, Chillingworth pretended not to know Lord Newburgh. He convinced the younger Elizabeth that it was shame and lack of courage that kept her from going to Lucius' house, telling her that if she went, she might have a Catholic accompany her.

Eventually, Chillingworth was discovered to be a fraud. Within days of claiming an oath of allegiance to the Catholic Church, he put in writing his thought that Roman Catholics should be held as heretics by the Church of England, stating that he would prove them so. As Elizabeth's daughter wrote of Chillingworth, "his tale hung not well together in many things." After coming twice more to the Cary household, he departed, this time to the house of Lucius.

Because Elizabeth's two youngest sons were visiting Lucius during a trip home from their boarding schools, she feared Chillingworth's effect upon them. Lucius did not claim to be anti-Catholic, but he had written several public papers that spoke against the faith. He explained this by saying he was simply investigating the topic, trying to learn more. While Lucius had never openly discussed his anti-Catholic feelings with his two young brothers, possibly out of deference to their mother, he had shown them these writings. Chillingworth supported Lucius' approach to religion by telling the boys that there was no certainty in any matter of religion.

While Elizabeth wanted to bring the young boys to live with her, she continued having difficulty in meeting financial responsibilities. Anne Cary liked to attend court, which meant Elizabeth had to furnish her with proper clothing, and all of the girls had needs Elizabeth attempted to fulfill. In addition, her household was ever changing. Some days she added another several mouths to feed, as she took in all who appealed to her for help. Although frail herself, and afflicted with a chronic cough, Elizabeth could never turn away a needy person.

Two years after Henry's death, Elizabeth again found herself nearly destitute. She even sold all of her bedroom furniture, except for a single chair in which she slept. Finally, Elizabeth had to ask Lucius to care for his sisters. She felt they were strong enough in their faith now that any effort to reconvert them would fail. During the time she lived with Lucius, Anne Cary decided to become a nun. Later, her sisters would make the same decision.

Although the separation from the children was difficult, the time alone allowed Elizabeth to regain both her strength and the courage to face her problems. Her daughters promised they would return to her as soon as possible.

Elizabeth withdrew from all of her business pursuits. In order to save money, she never used a carriage in the city and seldom left her house. When she did go out, she went on foot, something she'd not done when Henry was living and when her daughters were with her, so as not to embarrass them. She never borrowed money again, but asked friends for help whenever she required something which she could not purchase.

Her house was quiet during this time. She did receive a few Catholic friends and had visits from priests. But most of her time was spent reading.

But this period of calm was not to last long. She still wanted to find a way to bring all of her children home. She learned from her daughters that her two youngest sons, who had lived with Lucius most of their lives, had decided to convert to Catholicism. She grew determined to get them out of her eldest son's house.

Elizabeth asked for her daughters' help. They had to be very careful in their communications. Less than a year after they had moved in with their brother, two of Elizabeth's daughters and Lucius' wife, Lettice, came to visit Elizabeth in London. During the visit, Anne Cary told her mother that if the boys were not soon removed from Lucius' house, it would likely be impossible in the future. Elizabeth somehow managed to procure two horses and two men who agreed to carry out the plan of kidnaping her sons.

Elizabeth gave one of the men a note to pass to her daughters. The note instructed the girls to do whatever possible to help the boys, Patrick and Henry, leave the house in the company of the two men. The sisters then instructed the men to go from the house and wait a mile or so away. They warned the men that they would have to be patient.

After two or three days, Lucius finally left his house. Patrick and Henry had packed their belongings. The older sister told the household servants that the boys would be gone visiting the next day. The boys were so excited they got up at 3:00 a.m. on the day they were to leave.

Under cover of darkness, the boys met the men and crept down the road, escaping into the bushes when they heard a carriage coming. When they reached the river, they found their oarsman was drunk, which delayed their plans of crossing for the night. They were almost caught that night when the drunken man made it known to the local constable that the boys were "stolen children." Luckily, one of the men Elizabeth had hired knew the constable.

When Patrick and Henry reached London, Elizabeth hid them. Lucius had already scoured the countryside for his brothers upon finding them missing. When he discovered all of their belongings were gone, he knew their disappearance had been planned. He contacted his wife, who was in

Lucius Cary became a well-known English statesman.

London, asking her to search for them there. It must have bothered Lettice to do so, but she called upon Lord Newburgh, who was a member of the King's Council Table. The lordships called Elizabeth before them to ask what she knew of the boys' disappearance.

Elizabeth did not try to lie to the court officials, who had the authority to place her under arrest in the Tower of London. She told them she had sent for her children and then done what she thought was best. Even though she had been forced to "fetch them away" from their brother's house in secret, she felt she had broken no law. She protested that she could not be accused for taking what was her own, and that Lucius had never said he intended to keep the boys away from their mother.

Elizabeth had planned to send the boys to Europe for an education in a Catholic seminary, but they had not yet departed from London. So when the Council Table members accused her of illegally sending the boys to a Catholic seminary, she challenged them to prove such a charge. Elizabeth added that if the boys wanted to go to France for an education, she had a right to send them. The lords countered that to send them without permission was against the law. They had informed men at all ports not to let anyone pass without a license. This news didn't disturb Elizabeth, who replied that was no matter for her concern, but rather a matter for the men who had received the lords' directive. She herself had been issued no command. Likely exasperated by the logical arguments produced by Elizabeth, one council member asked if she intended to teach them the law. Elizabeth reminded them that she, being a lawyer's daughter, was not ignorant on the points of which they spoke.

They then demanded to know the name of the man who had removed Henry and Patrick from the country. When Elizabeth replied that she didn't know his name, they pointed out it wasn't likely she would turn over the care of her sons to a stranger. Then one man, Lord Chief Justice Bramston, was appointed to question Elizabeth in private. He was instructed that if not satisfied with her answers, he could send her to the Tower of London. During the interview, he confessed that he couldn't think of anything else to say to Elizabeth and offered her the use of his coach for her ride home.

The battle, however, was not yet over. Elizabeth set up a network of former servants to care for her sons a few days at a time. Each was questioned by the Council Table, and each could honestly say that he or she was only following their mistress' orders. When Lord Newburgh imprisoned one servant for two days, Elizabeth appeared at court and threatened to sue the statesman for false imprisonment. Lord Newburgh denied responsibility for the arrest, blaming it on the Lord Chief Justice, who also claimed to know nothing of the circumstance. At that point, the searches and questioning ceased.

Elizabeth's sons were educated in France at a Catholic seminary. Elizabeth could not afford the expenses required for such an education, but Queen Henrietta Maria contributed much of the needed money. Additional financial aid came from the priests in charge of training Henry and Patrick, as well as from other Catholic friends.

Soon after the boys departed London, the city was visited by one of the many plagues it suffered over the years. The deadly disease spread so quickly that those who could afford the expense left town until the danger of contracting the illness passed. Elizabeth moved the remainder of her children with her into the countryside, where they lived in two thatched huts for about six months.

Lucius remained unhappy with his mother for a time. The little communication that passed between them was in the form of letters in which each argued their own side. But about six months after his brothers were sneaked out of England, that changed. Lucius managed to redeem some of his father's property by paying off the mortgage, or debts, on the land. Well aware that he had disappointed his father by not marrying as Henry Cary had desired, Lucius felt he shouldn't benefit in any way from his father's estate. He decided to sell the property, then split the proceeds between his mother and his sisters and brothers. He contacted Elizabeth and asked her to meet with him so he could give her the funds. She immediately responded to him, asking for nothing except that his carriage be sent to pick her up. Lucius was so appreciative that they became friends again, and he saw that she was settled into better living quarters.

At last Elizabeth was at peace and could take up her writing once again. Over the next few months, she translated more of Cardinal Perron's works. She also enjoyed helping poor people find work spinning and sewing yarn and wool.

But before long, Elizabeth became very ill with the cough which had bothered her, according to her daughter, for over two decades. This series of "colds" was complicated by her not caring for her physical well-being. She likely had tuberculosis, which was called consumption in the seventeenth century. After becoming too sick to tend the disadvantaged any longer, she spent her time reading and writing, renewing her command of Hebrew and also of Latin by translating works written in those languages into English.

Over the following year, her daughters having matured and left her to become nuns, and her sons studying in Europe, Elizabeth lived alone. Once again she depended upon charity, but, as her daughter reported, never seemed to feel humiliation from the experience. When Lucius came to visit, Elizabeth managed to conceal her poor financial state. Eventually, he discovered the seriousness of her situation and gladly assisted his mother. Elizabeth did not want to burden her son, who had his own family expenses to pay. But Lucius remained loyal to his mother and asked his mother-in-law to look in on Elizabeth regularly to see that all of her needs were met.

In the final few months of her life, Elizabeth became very quiet and "easily ruled," according to her daughter. She had always expressed a terrible fear of death, but told a priest that she was now ready for it. She had seen six daughters become nuns, one son become a priest, and all of her surviving children except for Lucius convert to Catholicism. Although known as a difficult and stubborn woman, she also had a reputation for kindness and honesty and, of course, intelligence. Even though she had become so forgetful in the final months of her life that she might not recognize people she had known for years, she still found joy in her books and in writing. When Elizabeth Cary died in October of 1639, she left behind a heritage the worth of which would only be realized hundreds of years later.

CHAPTER NINE

Epilogue

Elizabeth Cary was buried in Queen Henrietta Maria's personal chapel. Fortunately, her death came before the English Civil War in which two of her sons, Lucius and Lorenzo, and Lucius' wife, Lettice, all died. At the time of his death, Lucius was well known in England as a statesman, writer and soldier. He was celebrated years later in a poem by the great eighteenth-century poet, Alexander Pope, as representative of the best young Englishmen sacrificed in the terrible war. Eventually, at least two biographies would be written about him.

While Elizabeth's daughters continued to serve the Catholic Church, her son Henry returned to England to study law. Patrick eventually left the priesthood to also study law in England, although he never achieved much success. Supported off and on by a royal pension, he published some poetry. Eventually, he married, and his son took up the title first granted to his grandfather, Henry Cary, becoming Lucius Henry Cary, the Sixth Viscount Falkland. Sometime between 1643 and 1649 a biography of Elizabeth was written by one of her daughters. Although the identity of the daughter is not known for sure, a later biographer of Elizabeth identified the author as Anne Cary, who was known after becoming a nun as Clementia.

Patrick Cary helped his sister by editing, or making corrections in, the biography. He wanted to remove passages which he believed were "too feminine," and he marked them through. Luckily, most of those passages were readable on the manuscript and have been printed in later editions of the biography. It remained in a French convent until it was published in 1861.

The confusion over the authorship of Elizabeth's play, *Mariam*, was due to its dedication to her sister-in-law who had the same name. It was eventually cleared up. But the confusion regarding her *History of Edward II* has lasted much longer. Because it was found among her husband's possessions, and was not published until 1680, the authorship was automatically credited to Henry Cary. There was little evidence that Henry had written the book. So few copies of the history exist that it can only be found among rare book collections in university libraries. In the coming

This statuette celebrates the religious aspect of Elizabeth Cary's complex personality.

decades, some scholar may take on the job of making the book available to the public. However, this will require much work. Because it was written during a time when spelling was not yet consistent, and references were made to people and events which would be difficult to identify, such a project would be a major undertaking.

Even though *Mariam* has not been read much outside of the university setting, copies of it are available. One edition was released in 1994.

Anne's biography of Elizabeth Cary is a record of her life during a time few legal or personal records were kept. Because the biography was written by a daughter, all that it says can not be accepted. Her love and admiration for her mother may have caused her to represent Elizabeth in a more positive way than an uninvolved, or objective, biographer would. Much of the biography focuses upon Catholicism, understandable in view of the fact that the daughter was a Catholic nun. Still, the biography remains a remarkable historical record, one allowing modern readers insight into the life and activities of Elizabeth Cary.

Additional clues about Elizabeth and other obscure female writers of her time may be gained through dedications, like those by Michael Drayton and a poet named John Davies. These men lived and wrote at the same time as Elizabeth. Because Drayton's dedication mentions

Elizabeth's talent for learning languages, we know that information in her biography is true. And through Davies, the question regarding the authorship of *Mariam* was solved to the satisfaction of most scholars. He mentions that Elizabeth wrote a play set in Palestine, a description which matches *Mariam*'s setting. Then he refers to another of Elizabeth's dramas which was set in Syracuse. That play, along with so many writings by English Renaissance women, has never been found. They were lost or destroyed.

Only in the twentieth century did the importance of Elizabeth Tanfield Cary, the Viscountess Falkland, become clear. We can only wonder about the other women writers whose works have disappeared, or were never published. Hopefully, more evidence and manuscripts will be uncovered in the future. Until such discoveries are made, the lives and writings of other women, such as Elizabeth Cary, remain mysteries waiting to be solved.

TIMELINE

1585   Elizabeth Tanfield born in Oxfordshire, England.

1602   Elizabeth marries Henry Cary, Viscount Falkland.

1602-03 Range of dates during which time Elizabeth probably wrote *Mariam.*

1603   Death of Queen Elizabeth I, James VI of Scotland ascends to the throne as James I.

1605   Henry Cary captured in battle; he remains a prisoner in Spain for three years.

1609   Birth of Catherine, Elizabeth's first child.

1610   Birth of Lucius, Elizabeth's first son.

1612   Elizabeth's play "set in Palestine" mentioned in dedication by Sir John Davies.

1613   Publication of *The Tragedie of Mariam, the Faire Queene of Jewry.*

          Birth of son, Lorenzo (or Laurence).

1614   Birth of daughter, Victoria Cary.

1615   Birth of daughter, Anne Cary.

1616   Birth of son, Edward Cary (died in infancy).

1617   Birth of daughter, Elizabeth Cary.

1619   Birth of daughter, Lucy Cary.

1621   Birth of daughter, Mary Cary.

1622   Henry Cary begins service as lord deputy of Ireland.

1624   Birth of son, Patrick Cary.

1625   Death of James I; his son, Charles I, ascends to the throne.

          Birth of son, Henry Cary.

          Elizabeth leaves her husband in Ireland. Her conversion to Catholicism becomes public.

1627   Charles I places Elizabeth under house arrest. She petitions the King for permission not to live with her mother; requests that her husband be commanded to give her funds for support. Writes *The History of Edward II*.

1630   Elizabeth publishes her translation of the writings of Cardinal Perron with a dedication to the Queen, Henrietta Maria.

1633   Death of Henry Cary, Lord Viscount Falkland, following a hunting accident.

1636   Elizabeth arranges for her youngest sons to be kidnapped from the home of her eldest son, Lucius.

Defends her actions before the King's Council Table, which had the power to order her held prisoner in the Tower of London.

1639   Death of Elizabeth Cary, probably from tuberculosis.

1642   Outbreak of English Civil War.

1643-49 The *Life of the Lady Falkland* is written by one of Elizabeth's daughters.

1643   Lucius Cary, now the second Viscount Falkland, is killed at the battle of Newbury during the Civil War.

SOURCES

CHAPTER ONE
House Arrest
p.10   "To out-run those weary hours of deep and sad passion"
        Elizabeth Cary, *The History of the Life, Reign, and Death of
        Edward II, etc.* (J.C. for Charles Harper et. al., London,
        1660), Preface, [no page no].
p.11   ". . . it becometh not a maid to talk, where her father . . ."
        Elyot, Sir Thomas, ed. "The Defence of Good Women" in
        Vive's Instruction of a Christian Woman (London, 1540), 109.

CHAPTER TWO
A Girl of Much Spirit
p.17   "Woman's thought is swift, and for the most part . . ." Elyot,
        44.
p.18   ". . . is not certainly knowne whether it be compressed with
        the sea . . ." Kenneth C. Murdock, *The Sun at Noon: Three
        Biographical Sketches* (The Macmillan Company, New York,
        1939) 11.
p.18   ". . . liberty more than riches." Murdock, 11.
p.22   "The girl hath a spirit averse from Calvin." Barry F. Weller
        and Margaret W. Ferguson, eds., *The Tragedy of Mariam
        with the Lady Falkland Her Life by one of her daughters*
        (University of California Press, Berkeley, CA, 1994), 188.

p.24 "... adorned ... many rare perfections" "Sweete is the French tongue, . . ." Bernard D. Newdigate and Kathleen ` Tillotson, eds. *Michael Drayton & His Circle*. (Shakespeare Head Press, Oxford, 1941) 78.

CHAPTER FIVE
The Deed is Done
p.43 "... bright woman clothed in white having a crown on her head." Weller and Ferguson, 202.
p.44 "Well, I have you now in the court and here I will keep you" Weller and Ferguson, 204-05.
p.45 "The deed was done." Weller and Ferguson, 205.

CHAPTER SIX
The History of Edward II
p.48 "Whom now I may say I have long unhappily called wife." Richard Simpson, ed. *The Lady Falkland: Her Life from a ms. in the Imperial Archives at Lille*. (Catholic Publishing & Bookselling Company, Limited, London, 1861) 137.
p.48 "My desieirs wass I dout not . . ." Simpson, 146.
p.48 "Give me necessary means to feed and clothe me." Simpson, 144.
p.50 "Live quietly" Simpson, 138.
p.57 "... too great and deep a blemish . . ." Cary, *History of Edward II*, 129.
p.57 "I have not herein followed the dull Character . . ." Cary, *History of Edward II*, Preface [no page number].

CHAPTER SEVEN
Defending the Faith
p.60 "... a woeman, though farr above other woemen . . ." Weller and Ferguson, 171.
p.60 "... as a Catholic and a Woman . . ." Weller and Ferguson, 172.
p.61 "Rather too forward in borrowing." Weller and Ferguson, 214.
p.66 "Oh, softly!"Weller and Ferguson, 219.

INDEX

Abbot, George, 61
Anne, Queen of England, 33-34, 37

Boleyn, Anne, 20
Bramston, Lord Chief Justice, 79
Buckingham, Duke of, 46, 54-55

Calvin, John, 22-23, 33
Cary, Aldolphus, 32
Cary, Anne, 34, 74-75, 84, 86
Cary, Catherine, 33, 42-43
Cary, Edward, 34
Cary, Elizabeth (sister-in-law), 26
Cary, Elizabeth (daughter), 34
Cary, Elizabeth (Tanfield)
    birth and childhood, 15-18, 20, 22, 24
    education, 15-16, 22, 24
    as translator, 18, 20, 59-61, 81
    religious studies, 20, 22, 32-34, 38, 41-42, 44
    marriage, 25
    as writer, 10-12, 14, 26, 28-31, 53-54, 56-58, 60-61
    domestic life, 32-36, 38
    finances, 36, 44, 47-48, 50, 61-63, 74-75, 80-82
    in Ireland, 39-42
    as business woman, 39-41, 61-62, 74
    conversion to Catholicism, 9-10, 43-48
    house arrest, 9-10, 47
    loses children, 48
    relations with husband, 47-48, 50, 52, 62-63
    labeled as heretic, 61
    regains children, 63-64, 67
    death of Henry Cary, 66-67
    reputation as an intellectual, 68
    kidnaps sons, 68-69, 75-76, 78-80
    defends herself before Charles I, 71
    health problems, 36, 38, 74, 81
    before King's Council Table, 76, 78-79
    death, 82
    biography of, 84, 86
    confusion over authorship of works, 84, 86-87
    literary legacy, 84-87
Cary, Henry (grandson), 83-84
Cary, Henry, 9, 11, 25-26, 31-36,